Original title:
A Dream of the Tropics

Copyright © 2025 Creative Arts Management OÜ
All rights reserved.

Author: Julian Prescott
ISBN HARDBACK: 978-1-80581-636-2
ISBN PAPERBACK: 978-1-80581-163-3
ISBN EBOOK: 978-1-80581-636-2

Chorus of the Morning Rain

Raindrops dance on rooftops high,
Splashing giggles, oh my my!
The plants are singing, what a show,
While puddles jump like kids in tow.

Umbrellas twirl like crazy hats,
As folks skid by like happy rats.
With nature's laughter all around,
A silly scene in drops profound.

Palette of Island Hues

Colors splash like laughter bright,
On beaches where the sun takes flight.
Parrots gossip in shades so bold,
While coconuts tell tales of old.

The ocean winks with glimmering cheer,
Each wave a joke, come listen near.
Fishes flick like giggling sprites,
In waters warm with sunny bites.

Oasis of Forgotten Wishes

In a hammock caught in gentle sway,
Lies a turtle dreaming all day.
Palm trees gossip, whispers shared,
About the wishes no one dared.

Coconuts chuckle from their perch,
As ants line up for a tiny search.
Forgotten dreams, now play a game,
In the sunny spot where life's not tame.

Fables of the Whispering Winds

Winds curl stories through the trees,
Of cheeky monkeys and their knees.
They swing and laugh, a sight so grand,
While breezes tickle all the land.

The parrots chatter, sharing tales,
Of pirate ships and swaying sails.
In this funny land where dreams conspire,
Even the clouds can't help but admire.

Coral Reverie

Beneath the waves, I saw a fish,
Wearing a hat, it made a wish.
It swam with grace, a quirky ballet,
While crabs did the conga, hip-hip-hooray!

The shells all laughed, clapped with glee,
As sea turtles joined a conga spree.
With seaweed wigs and coral pearls,
They danced in circles, spinning twirls.

The Coconut Grove's Embrace

Coconuts drop, it's quite a show,
A nutty rain from trees that grow.
They bounce like balls, land with a plop,
And squirrels rush in, all ready to hop.

A parrot squawks, "I want to play!"
With a beak full of snacks, it steals the day.
Chasing tails in a playful chase,
Nature's own comedic grace!

Last Rays of a Polished Sunset

The sun dips low, a tangerine tease,
While crabs wear shades, enjoying the breeze.
A dog in flip-flops, what a sight,
Chasing fireflies, oh, what delight!

The sky turns pink, a cotton candy treat,
While lizards lounge, all laid-back and neat.
With endless giggles in the balmy air,
The evening whispers secrets without a care.

In the Shade of Hibiscus Blooms

Under the shade, a picnic planned,
Sandwiches dance, as if they've planned.
A beetle in shades sips nectar sweet,
While ants bring snacks, a tiny retreat.

The flowers giggle, colors so bright,
As the breeze plays tag, pure delight.
With laughter echoing, joy takes its flight,
Nature's funny way to close the night.

Essence of Joyful Laughter

Under the sun, we dance and sway,
Sipping coconuts, laughing all day.
Tiny crabs in a comical race,
Chasing their tails, they quicken the pace.

Fish in the ocean, they wiggle and twist,
Wearing sun hats made from seaweed mist.
A parrot yells jokes from trees up high,
While monkeys swing by, oh me, oh my!

Enshrouded in Tropical Splendor

On the beach, flip-flops on the sand,
Sunscreen goes flying from a careless hand.
Palm trees chuckle with the winds that blow,
As tourists slip and fall in the glow.

Pineapples with legs, doing a jig,
Trying to dance all around a big fig.
Laughter erupts from a wave's big crash,
As surfboards collide with a silly splash.

Spectacle of the Tropical Night

Stars twinkle brightly in the inky sky,
Frogs serenade with their croaks nearby.
A firefly joins in the dance so bright,
While night critters put on a comical sight.

Giggles escape from the crickets below,
Their harmonies linger, putting on a show.
A turtle in shades moves with such flair,
Chasing his dreams without a single care.

Cascade of Sunset Starflowers

Sunset paints the sky in colors bold,
While giggling kids chase sunsets like gold.
Bouncing on waves like a rubber ball,
The ocean chuckles with a bubbly call.

As the last light fades, the laughter stays,
In the warm breeze, a cacophony plays.
Bamboos sway with glee, tapping their feet,
While crabs shake it off, what a silly feat!

Ballet of the Dancing Flames

In the garden the flames do sway,
While garden gnomes join the ballet.
Chasing shadows round the tree,
Laughing, twirling, wild and free.

The fireflies join in the fun,
Lighting up just like the sun.
One didn't mind a sizzling glance,
And did a wild electric dance.

Pineapple hats and coconut shoes,
As silly tunes drift in the hues.
The heat makes all a little daft,
Yet joy hangs like a tropical craft.

So if you see the flames take flight,
Join the jig, embrace the night.
Let the laughter bubble up high,
And twirl your friends beneath the sky.

Glistening Shores of Imagination

On shores where bright sea turtles race,
Sand castles grow a funny face.
A crab steals fries right off the plate,
While giggling fish discuss their fate.

Seagulls squawk in silly songs,
As kids build towers, oh so strong.
A coconut drops, causing a mess,
And everyone laughs at the dress.

The sun smiles wide, showing its teeth,
While mermaids swim with a playful wreath.
They toss their tails, creating a splash,
Surprising the tourists in a flash.

In dreams where sand and jokes collide,
With giggles where the waves abide,
We dance among the breeze and foam,
In this land we call our home.

Cascading Dreams of Paradise

Drinking juice from giant fruits,
The monkeys wear their silly boots.
They swing and twirl from tree to tree,
Chasing each other, full of glee.

Waterfalls laugh with whispered cheers,
Tickling toes as joy appears.
Splashing suddenly out of the shade,
A giant fish in a bright parade.

Fluffy clouds begin to play,
Hiding the sun in a fluffy way.
They change to shapes, a zebra here,
A cake with candles, oh so near.

With chuckles echoing in the haze,
We embrace these whimsical days.
Among the laughter, we'll forever stay,
In paradise, come what may.

Journal of a Sun-kissed Heart

Oh, the sun slipped on its shades,
And danced on the leaves so green,
A coconut grin on its face,
It pointed at me, so keen.

With pineapple hats in great pride,
The parrots all took to snickering,
As mangoes rolled down the slide,
Oh, the laughter, just like a swing!

A flamingo with socks squeezed tight,
Juggled lemons under the sun,
While I tossed my dreams in flight,
Hoping all this fun won't shun.

At dusk, the crabs held their show,
Tap-dancing in the warm sand,
I joined in with a silly toe,
As we all formed a crabby band.

Refrain of Cinnamon Skies

At noon the clouds wore candy stripes,
Swaying like hula in the breeze,
A piña colada full of vibes,
Laughing with each warm tease.

The sun winked, a cheeky lad,
While coconuts played peek-a-boo,
Bananas slipped, oh what a fad,
Chasing dreams in joyful hue.

Birds sang out in musical jest,
A chorus filled with goofy glee,
The palms swayed, they loved the fest,
Tickled by the waves carefree.

Even the fish wore silly hats,
As they splashed in the sunset glow,
Creating a splash with their chats,
In a world of sweet, silly show.

Songs of the Tropical Dawn

The sun arose like a sleepy cat,
Stretching out over the sandy bay,
A chicken then tried to play pat,
With the unsuspecting ray!

With citrus kisses on my cheek,
The waves murmured jokes quite bright,
While a lizard in shades whispered sneak,
"Morning, let's giggle in light."

Seashells sang their clam-like tunes,
While the surf laughed like a clown,
Frolicking under the puffy moons,
As I swayed with my goofy gown.

The iguanas dressed up for fun,
In tiny bowties, sharp and neat,
They boogied till the day was done,
Chasing dreams with two left feet.

Festivals of Fragrant Petals

A parade of blooms in paradise,
With daisies all decked like royalty,
Laughing bees caught in a spice,
   Sharing giggles in total glee.

The hibiscus wore a carnival hat,
While the orchids spun in delight,
A lizard pranced around like a brat,
   Chasing hues in a playful flight.

Confetti of petals filled the air,
As butterflies danced with a grin,
In a world with joy all to share,
   Letting silliness begin!

Twinkle lights in the guava trees,
Turned the night into a grand ball,
Amidst the laughter of the breeze,
We twirled around, we had a ball.

Tranquil Spaces under the Palms

Beneath the palms, a chair that squeaks,
I nibble fruits, while my stomach peaks.
The seagulls squawk, a true French flair,
As I spill my drink, with a careless air.

A lizard struts, with style and grace,
I try to dance, but trip on my lace.
They sip their drinks, while I make a scene,
Why does the beach make me a clownish queen?

Blooming Shores of Hope

The flowers bloom, but so do my woes,
I wedged my toe where the rooster goes.
A crab walks by, in official attire,
I'm calling for help, but it won't inquire.

The sun is bright, and the sand feels hot,
I saw a hat wave, but it was just a pot.
The breeze whispers secrets, tickles my ear,
Then sand in my shorts proves I live here!

Glimmers of Freedom by the Sea

The waves crash loud, a mocking delight,
I tried to swim, but got tangled in plight.
My sunscreen's a mess, like a crafty art,
A seagull's laughter, oh, it breaks my heart.

I built a sandcastle, quite grand and tall,
Only to watch as it starts to fall.
The tide rolls in, that sneaky beast,
But I'll hold my ground, at least for a feast!

Vibrancy of Life in Full Color

The colors pop, like a wild piñata,
Where'd that pinched shrimp meet the cool agua?
A parrot squawks, with a quip so wise,
While I juggle coconuts, just to surprise.

With cocktails all served, I give them a toast,
I toast a tall palm, and declare it my host.
The day rolls on, with giggles and cheer,
As life blooms here, just don't call it mere!

Island Whispers

Under the sun, a crab does dance,
With tiny legs, it takes a chance.
Seagulls squawk, they steal my fries,
Wearing beach hats, oh what a guise!

Coconut drinks with festive straws,
I sip and giggle, find my flaws.
A parrot talks, with a cheeky grin,
It tells my secrets, oh where to begin!

Beneath the Canopy

A monkey swings with style and flair,
Grabbing my hat, oh how rude, I swear!
Tiki torches flicker, night creeps in,
I giggle as the iguana grins.

Chasing fireflies, oh what a plight,
They twinkle and tease, such mischievous light.
The night is a symphony, a funny tune,
Dancing with shadows beneath the moon.

Swaying Palms and Starlit Skies

Palms sway gently, whispering laughs,
While I trip on sand, nobody has gaffs.
The stars in the sky play peekaboo,
With a wink and a nod, they just might too!

Crabs have parties, they're quite the sight,
Clinking their shells with all their might.
I join in the fun with a silly dance,
And trip over shells, oh what a chance!

Lullabies of the Ocean

The tide rolls in with a bubbly laugh,
Waves chase my toes, it's a foot bath.
  Fish play hide and seek with glee,
   While I splash water, getting free!

Shells whisper tales of days gone by,
  I pretend to listen, oh my oh my.
The ocean croons a lullaby sweet,
As I laugh at crabs shuffling their feet.

Elysium Found in Every Drop

Raindrops dance on coconut trees,
They giggle as they fall with ease.
A splash of joy, a burst of cheer,
Wet swimsuits bring the beach quite near.

Sunshine rainbows sprout from sand,
Tropical birds form a silly band.
Chasing crabs that wiggle and dart,
A lively game brings sunshine to heart.

Treasure of the Distant Shores

Pirate ships with wobbly sails,
Chasing fish with very short tales.
A treasure map that leads to snacks,
Chocolate coconuts, no time to relax.

Mermaids giggle, spinning about,
Tangled in nets they cry out,
"Don't pull us up, we'll share our fries!"
Who knew the sea holds such surprise?

Drifting into Serene Horizons

A hammock sways, my thoughts take flight,
Coconuts whirl in a dance so light.
Snoring cats beneath the sun,
Even they know life's just for fun.

Clouds shaped like dragons drifting by,
Whispering secrets to the sky.
Surfboards ride waves that giggle and tease,
"Catch me if you can, I'm the breeze!"

Mosaic of Colorful Canopy

Vines that tickle, roots that play,
Lizards in shades of bright ballet.
Each flower laughs in vibrant hues,
A parade of laughter, too many to choose.

Silly monkeys swing by in glee,
Winking at us from their tree.
Banana peels placed near my feet,
"I'm catching you next time, try not to cheat!"

Nectarous Breezes of the Isles

In the sun, the chickens dance,
While coconuts begin to prance.
Palm trees giggle in the wind,
Whispering secrets, never pinned.

Mangoes roll like giggling kids,
Avoiding all the playful squids.
Sandy toes and cheerful cheers,
Even crabs wear funky gears.

Lemonade spills, a salty splash,
The beach ball flies, an awkward crash.
Fish are swimming in their suits,
While glee fills every pair of boots.

Laughter echoes like a song,
Here in paradise, we belong.
With every joke, the sun will rise,
In this place of sweet surprise.

Gentle Murmurs of Hidden Coves

Underneath a warm cocoon,
The beach bum sings a silly tune.
Seagulls cackle, stealing fries,
As sunbathed folks engage in sighs.

Shells gather gossip, quite absurd,
Whispers dance without a word.
Snorkelers snicker at the fish,
Who float past like a dreamy wish.

Clouds wiggle in the vibrant blue,
As snorkel masks look on askew.
Jumping waves in rainbow hues,
Rollicking laughter, joyful views.

Tans grow bold like daring tales,
While ice cream cones become our sails.
In these nooks, we play and roam,
Every wave feels like our home.

Tides of Yearning in the Sun

Sandy toes and ice-cream bliss,
Waves crash for a goofy kiss.
The sun wears shades, quite the sight,
As flip-flops tango, oh so light.

Jet skis zoom with wild delights,
While seagulls join the daring flights.
Parrots squawk their stand-up bits,
As laughter fills the warm sunlit bits.

A crab takes center stage with flair,
While sunscreens wage a winning dare.
Determined tan lines draw the crowd,
With every joke, we laugh aloud.

In this fun fair of salty dreams,
Where nothing's ever as it seems.
The tides of joy pull us along,
In this quirky, sunny song.

Horizon's Edge in Tropical Embrace

On the horizon, llamas leap,
With juicy fruits, in piles they steep.
Mango madness in the breeze,
As coconuts roll with such ease.

Cocktails with umbrellas sway,
While turtles join the dance and play.
The sun sets with a wink and jig,
As the night comes, we all dig.

Silly hats and swimming trunks,
As conch shells sing their playful flunks.
Stars above twinkle like our glee,
In this wild, hilarious spree.

The night unfolds with laughter loud,
While crickets chirp and join the crowd.
In this embrace, we pitch a tent,
Creating memories, love well-spent.

Lush Green Soliloquy

In the jungle, a vine does sway,
A monkey shows off his ballet.
With leaves that wiggle all around,
He takes a bow, very profound.

The parrot squawks a silly tune,
While sipping nectar from a bloom.
The sloth rolls by, oh so slow,
He thinks he's won the world's big show.

A frog jumps high, in the air, he's set,
Landing on a coconut, what a bet!
He croaks a joke that's hard to catch,
His friends all laugh, what a mismatched batch!

The sun dips low, it's time for bed,
But no one's tired, not a shred.
Nighttime comes with a funny twist,
The forest giggles, can't resist!

Cerulean Dreams

The ocean waves don a broad smile,
With fish that swim in goofy style.
A dolphin jumps with a flip and twirl,
Saying, "Watch me!" to the salty whirl.

Seagulls squawk, they're quite the crew,
Stealing chips from tourists, it's true!
A crab dances sideways, oh what a sight,
Shuffling in sand with sheer delight!

In the distance, a hammock swings,
Beneath a sky where laughter rings.
A lobster waves from a nearby rock,
Shouting, "The beach is a funny clock!"

As evening falls, the sunset glows,
The horizon wears a vibrant rose.
But the fish are still throwing a fuss,
Launching popcorn all over the bus!

An Evening with the Fireflies

The night is lit by tiny sparks,
Dancing like crazy in the parks.
Fireflies wear their golden attire,
Winking at folks, they never tire.

"Catch me if you can!" they tease,
Flitting about with such great ease.
A cat stalks on the prowl, just shy,
The fireflies laugh and zip on by.

A picnic spread on the soft grass,
With lemonade served in a glass.
The bugs join in, it's quite a crowd,
They twinkle brightly, feeling proud!

As midnight strikes, the fun won't quit,
The stars above give a gentle wit.
Together they dance till the dawn does break,
A whimsical party by the lake!

Driftwood Reflections

On the shore, a driftwood log waits,
Listening to the sea, with jokes it creates.
A crab scuttles and offers a pun,
"Why did the fish not want to run?"

The log just chuckles, "Oh dear friend,
Just think of the waves, they never end!"
Waves crash softly, the ocean grins,
As sandcastles tumble, it joyfully spins.

A pelican glides, looking for lunch,
He miscalculates, oh what a crunch!
"Too slippery!" he quips, as he flies away,
Leaving the seagulls in dismay.

As day turns to night, the log stays tight,
Sharing sea tales under the moonlight.
With laughter and splashes, the stories flow,
In this quirky kingdom of ebb and glow!

Caress of the Island Air

The breeze tickles my nose, oh dear,
A coconut falls, and I fear!
With flip-flops flapping, I jog in place,
In search of a smoothie, my lips to grace.

Lumps of sand stuck to my toes,
Sunburned smiles from my forehead flows.
Umbrellas up high like candy canes,
As seagulls laugh at my sunburned pains.

I dance with a crab, a wobbly foe,
He sidesteps sideways, putting on a show.
The palm trees sway as if to tease,
Whispering secrets on a playful breeze.

A mango splatters upon my head,
I chuckle and laugh, no time for dread.
In this sunny mess, life is a treat,
Even the lizards tap dance on the street.

Canvas of Coral Dreams

The fish wear colors that can't be named,
Each splash a laugh, no one feels ashamed.
A sea turtle glides, gives a nod and grin,
While starfish giggle as they slow spin.

Corals pretend they're an art gallery,
With jellyfish floating, light and airy.
I tried to dive, but my flip-flops stuck,
Now I'm the treasure, in this odd luck.

I thought I found a pearl, so bright,
Turned out a clam with a goofy bite.
In this underwater circus we play,
Life flips and flops like a fish on a tray.

Nemo waves while a whale plays the flute,
I dance like seaweed, but my moves are moot.
Amidst the chaos of bubbles and glee,
This watery world is the best place to be.

Luminescence of Starry Nights

Underneath stars, we roast marshmallow dreams,
With laughter that bursts, it bubbles and beams.
The moon grins wide, a silly ol' chap,
As we trip on shadows, sharing a nap.

A crab in a tux, with a top hat on,
Claps its claws to the night's sweet song.
Fireflies dance like they've lost their wits,
And I begin to wonder, where's my wits?

The ocean sings, a sloshy ol' tune,
While I'm stuck in a hammock, swaying like a loon.
I try to catch starlight in a jar,
But end up swatting at a mosquito subpar.

Dreams swirl like coconut pie in the air,
Life's just a giggle, devoid of despair.
With a wink from above, and soft sandy beds,
We drift into chuckles, resting our heads.

Garden of Exotic Longings

In a jungle full of giggles and bloom,
I chased a toucan, it laughed with a vroom.
Around the bend where the mango trees bend,
I found a gnome who loves to pretend.

Flowers wear hats, so brightly adorned,
Each petal a tale of adventures unscorned.
A lizard named Lou was playing checkers,
With butterflies who are notorious hecklers.

I tried to pluck a banana, oh what a sight,
It slipped from my fingers, gave me a fright.
As I tumbled down, the whole garden cheered,
A circus of laughter, my antics endeared.

Giggling frogs join in the parade,
Their croaks echoing, a raucous charade.
In this garden of quirks, I've truly found bliss,
Amongst the odd blooms, I've never felt missed.

Starlight Over a Quiet Lagoon

Stars are winking in the night,
Fish are dancing, feeling bright.
A crab walks sideways, but oh dear,
He thinks he's sliding, what a sheer!

Moonlit waters make jokes galore,
A turtle trips and starts to snore.
With every splash, there's laughter's tune,
The lagoon laughs beneath the moon.

An octopus plays peek-a-boo,
Hide and seek, who knew it too?
A seal attempts a fancy wave,
But belly flops, oh, what a save!

Count the fish in stripes and dots,
Are they playing or just tough tots?
In this lagoon, the fun floats free,
Beneath the starlit canopy.

Twilight within the Palm Fronds

At twilight's hush, the palms sway low,
A parrot sings, though tone's no show.
Underneath the leafy screens,
A gecko struts in shiny jeans.

The echo of a fruit bat's screech,
Frog leaps high, it's quite the breach.
Crickets chirp in chorus tight,
While fireflies twinkle, oh what a sight!

Bamboo sways with a gentle tease,
A monkey tumbles from the trees.
It lands with grace, or so it seems,
Then swings back up to join its dreams.

Laughter rolls past every trunk,
Each branch holds secrets, none debunked.
In this twilight, the fun unfolds,
As stories linger, carefree, bold.

Whispers of Palm Shadows

In shadows long, the palms will sway,
The sun peeks out to start the play.
A lizard grins, with sunburned fame,
Next to a frog who thinks he's game.

Crabs in the sand have their own dance,
Two-step across, oh what a chance!
Chasing each other, it's quite the scene,
But one slips and lands on a jellybean.

Waves giggle softly at the shore,
As a kitebird dives, then does a roar.
Back it flies, its wings ask for grace,
But lands on a kid's ice cream face!

With each palm whispering delight,
The day fades slowly into the night.
Under the stars, the laughter glows,
In those palm shadows, joy surely flows.

Enchantment by the Shore

The tide pulls back, a sly retreat,
A sandcastle stands on its tiny feet.
Seagulls gather, ready to feast,
On snacks stolen, they're quite the beast!

A clam chirps as the waves roll in,
While a kid dreams of a mermaid's fin.
But the mermaid's just a clever fish,
Who wiggles past with a cheeky swish.

As dusk arrives on the sandy plot,
A crab joins in, the silliest lot.
With clacking claws, they dance in glee,
While surfers shout, "Hey, look at me!"

Enchantment blooms where the shadows lay,
A flicker of stars marks the end of day.
In laughter's echo, the night comes alive,
At the shore where silly dreams thrive.

Labyrinth of Verdant Paths

In jungle mazes, where I roam,
I tripped on vines and said, "I'm home!"
The trees all laughed, they knew my fate,
I'd dine on bugs and feel quite great.

A parrot squawked, "Oh what a sight!"
As I danced with my friend, the knight.
Coconut drinks spilled down my chin,
A slippery way to find my win!

The path was long, my feet grew sore,
But who needs shoes when you've got more?
A frog croaked tunes, my dance partner,
We made quite the show, a green superstar!

So if you wander, keep this thought,
In jungles wide, fun's all you've sought.
With every twist, a laugh ensues,
In the labyrinth, you'll lose your blues.

When Mangoes Ripen

Beneath the sun, I hear them call,
Those juicy gems that dare to fall.
I climbed a tree, oh what a climb,
But slipped right off, like slippery slime!

A mango rolled and hit a goat,
He snorted loud, my silly hope.
"Hey buddy!" I cried out in haste,
He said, "No fruit, you're such a waste!"

We made a pact, in fruit we trust,
To dodge the bees and eat what's just.
But mangoes flew from every nook,
Now goats and I write mango books!

So if you're hungry, make sure to share,
With goats galore, no mango's spare.
Together we feast, the sun our guide,
In fruity bliss, we take our ride.

Wildflowers in a Tropical Dawn

Amidst the blooms, I woke with glee,
A bee flew by and buzzed with me.
The daisies giggled, swaying slow,
Said, "Let's all dance, put on a show!"

The sun peeked in with a sleepy yawn,
As I twirled 'round, my breakfast dawned.
Pineapples rolled like children free,
Singing along with every bee.

Lizards joined in, with scaly flair,
They completed my grand floral affair.
Chasing shadows, we played all day,
In vibrant colors, we lost our way!

So if you wake in flowered delight,
Join the parade of morning light.
With nature's giggles in every hue,
You'll laugh until the day is through.

The Spirit of the Rainforest

In the depths where tall trees sway,
A spirit danced, hip-hip-hooray!
She twirled with vines, beneath the moon,
And sang a tune, a silly croon.

Monkeys swung in synchronized cheers,
They tossed around forgotten fears.
They thumped on drums made of big leaves,
While I just tried to keep my sleeves!

The jaguars chuckled, their spots a mess,
As I clumsily tried to impress.
With every step, I stomped and slipped,
And into a puddle, I promptly dipped!

But laughter echoed through the trees,
As nature grinned upon the breeze.
In this vibrant, silly, leafy show,
The spirit of joy begins to grow.

The Song of Cascading Waterfalls

The water sings a tune, oh dear,
It splashes up, then disappears!
A fish just winked, how very bold,
In this mad dance, the fun unfolds.

Lemurs swing, with grace, they leap,
A monkey steals my snack, the creep!
I chase him down, slip on a vine,
Laughing at chaos, it feels divine.

The palm trees sway with rhythmic flair,
They seem to judge, they really stare.
With every slip, my friend just grins,
In this wild world, we're up for wins.

So here's a toast with coconut milk,
To all the laughs and mischief ilk!
Nature's stage, we've hit the floor,
In cascades of fun, we all explore.

Where the Tropics Breathe

The sun's so bright, I need a hat,
A lizard's lounging, imagine that!
With every buzz of gnats around,
I dance and spin, oh what a sound!

Palm trees rustle, what do they say?
'Keep your cool, it's a breezy day!'
But here I am, in a silly trance,
Trying to catch the wind's own dance.

A parrot squawks, with colors bold,
It mocks my hair, or so I'm told.
In this wild place, my worries flee,
Just me and laughs, that's the key!

So let the tropics weave their charm,
With playful breezes and endless calm.
In this realm of fun, so carefree,
I find my laughter, I just be.

Vows in the Tropical Mist

The mist is thick, can't see my friend,
Did he trip again, or just pretend?
With every giggle, the vow is made,
To never walk where the palm trees swayed.

A monkey steals my flip-flop shoe,
With every chase, my laughter grew.
In this hazy world, oh what a sight,
We pledge to make every day bright.

The flowers bloom, they seem to grin,
As if they know where we've been.
With petals swirling, we twirl and spin,
In tangled vows, let the fun begin!

So in this mist, let joy reside,
With silly antics, we coincide.
Every laugh a vow, it's true,
In this tropical love, just me and you.

A Flourish of Bougainvillea

Bougainvillea, bright and bold,
I've tripped on you, oh the story told!
In every color, a vibrant show,
They laugh at me, the flowers know.

With petals raining on my hat,
I dance around like a joyful brat.
The butterflies do their little spin,
As I struggle to keep my grin.

Palms wave along with every slip,
While I attempt a graceful dip.
With giggles echoing in the air,
I've become part of this floral fair!

So here's to blooms, with joy they bring,
And every fall that makes me sing.
In this vivid splash, I truly thrive,
Amongst the colors, I come alive!

Benevolent Monsoon Memories

Raindrops tap-dancing on my head,
I swayed like a palm in jest.
Each puddle a portal, laughter spread,
Welly-wearing revelers at their best.

Thunder grumbles, but who's afraid?
It's nature's way of making a splash!
With soggy socks, the fun's displayed,
As lightning makes the party flash.

Colors bloom in the mud galore,
Frogs croon their croaky refrain.
Sliding on leaves, who could want more?
Monsoon magic drives out the plain.

So bring the cake, and let's all cheer,
For rainstorms making spirits bright.
In the downpour, friendships adhere,
Benevolent storms, what a delight!

Dance of the Tropical Blossoms

Petals pirouette in the breeze,
Each one a tiny dancer bold.
With staff and score, they tease and please,
A floral ballet, pure gold!

Sunlight spills like honey sweet,
An audience of buzzing bees.
In their tiny seats, they tap their feet,
To the rhythm of swaying trees.

A banana tree steals the show,
With moves that twist and sway and twirl.
While hibiscus blooms put on a glow,
In a tropical whirl, a dizzy swirl!

So let's applaud the colors bright,
In a carnival of scented air.
Each blossom dances with pure delight,
A floral fiesta beyond compare!

Tides of the Lush Horizon

Coconuts bob like floaties in line,
As waves tickle sandy toes.
With a splash, I sip my fruity brine,
Balance on water—who knows how it goes?

Turtles race in their shells of green,
While crabs do their sideways sprint.
The ocean chuckles, a silly queen,
In its frothy laugh, I find a hint.

Surfers tumble, then rise with pride,
While gulls guffaw from above.
In this playground, no one can hide,
The tide's a joke we all love.

So let the waves carry our glee,
In buoyant bounces, so carefree.
Let's toast to the splashy spree,
Where horizons meet, absurdity!

Sweet Surrender to the Sunset

Sunsets melt like butter on bread,
Swirling colors in a funky mix.
As crickets chirp their twilight thread,
And fireflies dance with glowing tricks.

The horizon grins, a cheery face,
With oranges, pinks, and purples spry.
An evening's warmth, a warm embrace,
As day bows out with a playful sigh.

Laughter spills with the ocean's roar,
As shadows stretch and play charades.
While the crescent moon starts to soar,
In an encore of light, the world fades.

So raise a toast to the day's end,
With friends all gathered, not a care.
In every color, let joy blend,
Sweet surrender—this moment we share!

Serenade under the Mango Tree

Beneath the mango's leafy shade,
A parrot sings, a serenade.
The monkeys dance, in silly glee,
Chasing shadows, wild and free.

Lemons drop like little bombs,
While ants play band, with tiny drums.
The breeze tickles, makes us laugh,
As we sip juice from a coconut half.

A squirrel sways in rhythm fine,
While iguanas sip on brine.
In every jest, the skies a-blend,
Under the tree, where laughter's trend.

Oh, life is sweet, on this sunny show,
With fruit so ripe, and cheeks aglow.
In the land where comical dreams flow,
Join the fun, and let joy grow.

Echoes of Rainforest Heartbeats

In the forest, a symphony plays,
Frogs croak jokes in quirky ways.
The trees share secrets, old and wise,
While fireflies wink, a sweet surprise.

A sloth hangs low, in laughter's grip,
Waving slowly, with a silly flip.
Caterpillars form a funky line,
Strutting their stuff, like they're divine.

Echoes dance on a breezy tune,
While toucans shout; it's always noon.
Silly rains turn leaves to drums,
As nature's chorus hums and hums.

Oh, listen close, the heartbeats call,
Funny whispers rise, and fall.
In this vast green, where giggles start,
Every heartbeat, a merry art.

Sunlit Shores and Hidden Coves

On sunlit shores, the crabs parade,
In little hats, oh, what a charade!
Seagulls cackle, gossip afloat,
As dolphins perform on a wobbly boat.

Shells giggle as they roll in line,
While kids play tag and sip on brine.
A beach ball bounces, chases the sun,
With laughter echoing, oh, what fun!

Hidden coves with treasures untold,
Where seaweed dances, bright and bold.
A starfish grins, a cheeky smile,
As we splash around, in the ocean's aisle.

Oh, the tales that the waves can weave,
With salty winds that tickle and tease.
In this lazy paradise, we believe,
Laughter's a wave that will never leave.

Ballad of the Tropical Breeze

The tropical breeze comes swaying by,
With a giggle and a gentle sigh.
It carries whispers from the trees,
And teases flowers, 'Oh, if you please!'

Coconuts roll like merry balls,
While palm fronds sway and take the calls.
A lizard grins on a fence post tall,
Sipping lemonade, sharing a brawl.

The breeze tells tales of surf and sun,
Of quirky creatures, having fun.
With every swoosh, it sings a song,
Of joyful hearts, where we belong.

So when you feel that playful air,
Join in the dance, without a care.
Let laughter lift you, light as a feather,
In this warm world, we're all together.

Echoes of the Sapphire Sea

There once was a crab with a hat,
He fancied himself quite the aristocrat.
But when the tide rolled in,
His hat took a spin,
And he danced like a fool on the mat.

A dolphin joined in for a laugh,
With a flip and a splash like a gaffe.
They wiggled and giggled,
All troubles were jiggled,
In the ocean where joy's the best half.

A fish wearing glasses swam by,
Claiming he'd read 'War and Peace' high.
But with each little flip,
He lost all his grip,
And forgot every word, oh my!

So raise up your glass to the sea,
Where silliness flows wild and free.
For laughter's the key,
In this world by the sea,
As we prance with pure glee, whee!

Lullabies Beneath the Coconut Trees

Under the palms, a monkey swung,
His lullabies sweetly were sung.
But when he lost track,
And fell with a whack,
His tunes turned to just bongo drums, sprung.

A parrot squawked with delight,
"Hey buddy, your singing's a fright!"
With feathers in disarray,
He danced all the day,
Pulsing rhythms beneath stars so bright.

The crickets began their own jam,
They brought out a tiny grand slam.
But their beats went astray,
In a bizarre ballet,
Now it's chaos and not just a glam.

As night blankets all in its haze,
We chuckle and share silly ways.
In this tropical cheer,
Bringing laughter and beer,
We hug our sweet dreams as it plays.

Mirage of Paradise

In a land where the sun loves to tease,
A lizard croaked out with great ease.
"Watch me do the split,
It's quite a neat trick!"
And landed right on top of some bees.

A toucan tried out for a show,
With a one-man band putting on a glow.
But a hiccup so loud,
Brought a startled crowd,
And he ended up playing the low.

The flowers began to take flight,
Each bloom was a fluttering sight.
They giggled with glee,
Spreading joy so carefree,
As they danced in the warm, silly night.

In this mirage of laughter and fun,
Where each day feels like a bright run,
With creatures that play,
In a whimsical way,
We frolic together, everyone!

Rhythms of the Warm Breeze

The wind whispered secrets to trees,
As a turtle slid down with great ease.
He claimed he could fly,
As he burst from the sky,
But just landed with a soft 'please'.

A flamingo struck poses with flair,
"Look at my dance, if you dare!"
But tripped on a leaf,
Causing such grief,
He ended up stuck in the air.

While sandcastles debated their plan,
As they challenged each wave with a span.
When a crab swam by,
Feeling quite spry,
He declared he was the king of the sand!

In this world where the silly finds space,
Join the folly, and pick up the pace.
Bring laughter and song,
Join the merry throng,
As we bask in this carefree embrace!

Oasis of the Untamed Night

In the land where coconuts play,
The parrots dance through the day.
A toucan with a silly grin,
Claims he's the king, let the fun begin!

Under stars that twinkle bright,
The monkeys swing with sheer delight.
One steals a hat, thinks it's a crown,
While the flamingos strut all around.

The crabs are hosting a moonlit feast,
Inviting all from the very least.
The sandcastles tumble with laughter loud,
As the sea turtles wear them proud.

So grab a drink from the coconut shell,
Join the party, oh do not dwell.
In this oasis, joy takes flight,
Where every moment feels just right!

Skylines Beyond the Palms

Between the leaves, a skyline peeks,
Where iguanas gossip and parakeets speak.
Every sunset brings a glowing cheek,
As shadows stretch, the night goes bleak.

A hammock sways beneath the stars,
With laughter echoing from nearby bars.
The flamingos play a game of chase,
With a pelican flying out of place.

Tiki torches flicker in the breeze,
While sea turtles join with utmost ease.
A pineapple served on a plate so grand,
Brings a smile to every sun-kissed hand.

So raise a toast to this vibrant scene,
With every drink, let your heart lean.
For in the laughter among the palms,
Lies a magic that forever calms.

Twilight Reflections from the Gulf

Under the moon, the waters gleam,
As a fish jumps out with a silly beam.
A seagull squawks with quite the flair,
Claiming he's the star of this seaside fair.

The tides tickle, like a playful tease,
While crabs scuttle with prancing knees.
A dolphin pops up to join the fun,
Winking at the moon, oh what a run!

The beach is alive with giggles and cheer,
As shells whisper secrets for all to hear.
Stars are the audience, shining bright,
While the ocean dances into the night.

So come take a dip in twilight's glow,
Join in the laughter, let spirits flow.
With each splash, conjure a merry thrill,
In this sleepy gulf that always will.

Hush of Enchanted Waters

In whispers soft, the waters sing,
Where turtles wear the ocean's bling.
They twirl and swirl in a graceful flow,
While a starfish shares some tales below.

The wandering breeze joins in the jest,
As sea urchins turn at the ocean's behest.
A crab in a bowtie lounges on sand,
Claiming it's the best view in the land.

Driftwood chairs in a sun-kissed row,
Where every tale brings a hearty glow.
The sea grapes giggle as waves come in,
Playing tag with the waves, let the fun begin!

So float along in this watery cheer,
Embrace the laughter, hold it dear.
For in the hush of these enchanted shores,
Adventure awaits, behind ocean doors!

Flight of the Elusive Bird

A parrot with a heart-shaped nose,
Wears fruit hats, everybody knows.
He dances with a mango twist,
In the shade where sunlight kissed.

With wings so wide and thoughts so grand,
He lands atop a giant stand.
Chasing shadows, gaining speed,
He giggles at a swarming bead.

He flaps around, a silly sight,
Scribbles notes in colors bright.
As he chirps a tune so loud,
A coconut falls - what a crowd!

It's laughter that he brings to all,
A clownish bounce on nature's ball.
In this kingdom of sunlit mirth,
He reigns supreme, our laugh-filled earth.

Tapestry of Brightly Bloomed Dreams

In gardens where the daisies prance,
A gnome does the hilarious dance.
His red hat bobbing, full of cheer,
Tripping on roots, oh dear, oh dear!

Butterflies whisper in the breeze,
While he trips over honeybees.
They giggle, saying, 'Oh, what fun!'
As he stumbles under the sun.

Flowers chatter, color-bursting,
With petals ripe for hijinks thirsting.
The roses laugh with tiny throats,
As gnomes wear pants made of old coats.

What a scene of uproarious sway,
In blooms that laugh and twist all day.
Join the gnome in his silly reverie,
Where petals party with wild harmony!

Silhouettes Against a Golden Ray

Lizards lounge in evening light,
Explaining jokes in their own sight.
With tails that twitch and colors flash,
They share some laughs before the splash.

A crab recites a stand-up skit,
While waves applaud, not one bit quit.
His claws are snapping, what a hit,
As seagulls laugh, 'Oh, isn't it!'

Sky and sea have formed a scene,
With salty jokes that make them lean.
Against the sun, silhouettes sway,
In a world where laughter finds a way.

As the tide rolls in, don't you see?
That even shells are full of glee.
With echoes that will never fade,
In this bright tale, joy's masquerade!

Land of Forgotten Chants

In a land where shadows joke and play,
Old palm trees dance, come what may.
With rusty crows on rusty swings,
They croon out tunes of wondrous things.

A turtle sings an off-pitch song,
About the days that felt so long.
Yet, all the fish are in the know,
They splash around with gleeful flow.

With echoes carried on the breeze,
And laughter blending through the trees,
The jests of yore await the bold,
In this wild land of tales retold.

So grab a seat, and join the fun,
In a quirky place where dreams have spun.
With chants forgotten, yet still alive,
Together we'll dance, and laugh, and thrive!

The Call of Singing Seashells

On the shore, shells start to hum,
Crabs dance like they're at a drum.
Turtles wear shades, looking quite cool,
While starfish gather around the pool.

Seashells sing songs, off-key but loud,
They're the weirdest, wiggliest crowd.
A seagull joins in, a real diva,
Chasing fish with flair, in a real wild fever.

The waves do a jig, splashing with glee,
While limpets plunge into a spree.
Hermit crabs scuttle, just don't tell,
Each has a plan to ring the bell.

Sunset cheers as the night descends,
Fish wear tutus, as laughter blends.
In this quirky place, let worries cease,
Join the chorus, feel the peace!

Echoes of the Island's Heart

A coconut falls, thud with a laugh,
Monkeys swing by, taking a gaff.
Parrots squawk jokes, sharp as a whip,
While tourists attempt their comedy trip.

Bamboo sways, whispering a tune,
Lemurs groove to the rising moon.
Raccoons in shades, stylish and neat,
Stealing snacks, oh what a feat!

The island's pulse beats with delight,
Frogs in bow ties hop left and right.
A pineapple rolls, what a grand show,
It seems even fruit likes to go with the flow.

In this merry place, where giggles abound,
Nature's chuckles are all around.
Join the fun, let worries depart,
Feel the echoes of this island's heart!

Journey Through the Green Veil

Through the jungle, vines do twirl,
Monkeys leap, giving a whirl.
A lizard grins, in a top hat,
While moths on a dance floor do chat.

A parrot talks, "What's up, dear friend?"
"Got any snacks? The fun won't end!"
Butterflies in gowns flit with grace,
Each finds its rhythm in this wild race.

The trees tell tales, of olden days,
While toucans toast with fruity bays.
Cameramen fumble to catch that flight,
As a sloth waves, "I'll join you tonight!"

This ride through green is quite the scene,
Laughter echoes, a joyful glean.
So grab your hat, with the sun on the trail,
Join this wacky, wild green veil!

Flickers from the Lantern-lit Docks

Lanterns sway, making shadows play,
Fishermen dance the twilight away.
Crabs in tuxedos take center stage,
A fishing boat turns into a page.

The moon winks, with a cheeky grin,
As octopuses bring their violin.
Mackerels challenge for the best song,
Their scales shimmer, dazzling and strong.

Eyes wide open, wonders in tow,
A jellyfish shows off its bright glow.
The night's crescendo reaches its peak,
In this zany corner, let laughter sneak.

With each flicker, the night grows bold,
Creating stories of laughter told.
Join the dock, where joy isn't rare,
And dance with the night—a vibrant affair!

Flavors of the Warm Ocean Breeze

Coconut laughs as it rolls off the shelf,
Pineapple smiles, says, "Hey, how about some help?"
Mango wiggles, dances in the sun,
"Forget the diet, let's have some fun!"

The sea salt tickles my nose with a grin,
Lime joins the party, says, "Let's all dive in!"
With each tropical flavor, we jump and we twirl,
Ignoring the world, just a sweet, juicy swirl!

The guava winks, enticing and bright,
While bananas slip off in sheer delight.
Fruits having fun as they burst and they play,
In a carnival feast, we'll laugh all the way!

A conch shell whistles, drawing us near,
It tells the tales of both laughter and cheer.
In this sweet paradise, all flavors agree,
Life is a party, come savor with me!

Vibrations of the Night Market

Lanterns shimmer like starry eyes,
As vendors shout their playful surprise.
Fried dough twirls with a laugh in the air,
While sticky rice giggles without any care.

Carts roll and bump with a rhythmic beat,
Coriander dances on spicy street feet.
Samosas chuckle, hot from the pan,
While tourists wander, led by the plan.

The rich curry sings in a sizzling voice,
Tempting the sauces, oh how we rejoice!
Lemonade zing, sharp as a dart,
Making us giggle, right from the start.

In this market, every flavor's a joke,
With laughter and spices, they blend and they poke.
Eating our way through the whims of the night,
In a feast of joy, everything feels right!

Mystique of the Velvet Sand

Velvet grains play hide and seek,
Tickling toes, oh what a peak!
The sun shimmies, a golden dance,
As jellyfish prance in a curious trance.

Crabs wear hats, looking so sly,
Chasing each other, oh my, oh my!
Seagulls call with a cheeky cheer,
Saying, "Join the fun, come dive down here!"

Footprints giggle, tracing their way,
In the sands where silly shadows play.
A beach ball bounces, a joyful jest,
As waves take turns for a playful quest.

Here, the sand whispers secrets untold,
Of treasures and tales, of new and of old.
With a laugh and a splash, we roam hand in hand,
In the mystique that lies in the velvet sand.

Portals to the Exotic Eras

Timeless parrots with ribbons so bright,
Squawk ancient secrets in colorful flight.
Palm trees sway, with a knowing glance,
As time travelers join in the dance.

Lost in the laughter of days long past,
With tofu that jiggles and lasts none too fast.
Sipping on juices, both sharp and sweet,
We munch on star fruits, a rare little treat.

The spices swirl, a fragrant delight,
Bringing back memories from each night.
With a wink of the eye, and a cheeky cheer,
We toast to the past, each party's near!

In this quirky daydream, all eras collide,
With playful adventures, we take in our stride.
Every flavor we taste spins a tale all its own,
In portals of joy, we happily roam!

Elixir of Island Hues

In shades of lime and mango, bright,
The drinks we sip bring pure delight.
With tiny umbrellas swaying free,
We toast to life beneath the tree.

The parrots gossip, loud and bold,
As sunburned tourists seek the gold.
A dance-off in the sand ensues,
With laughter echoing through our shoes.

The ocean waves, they tickle toes,
While seashells hide, in sneaky rows.
We chase the crabs, they scuttle fast,
In this fine paradise, we'll ever last.

So raise a glass to fruity fun,
Where all is bright, and we all run.
In brilliant colors, we are schooled,
As joy by nature's hand is ruled.

Dimensions of the Coconut Grove

Beneath the palms, we seek some shade,
Protection from the sun's crusade.
A squirrel steals a slice of pie,
While we enjoy a warm goodbye.

The coconuts, like heads on high,
Are plotting schemes to make us sigh.
A gentle breeze, a ruffled hat,
Leaves us puzzled, wondering 'what was that?'

Picnics spread, all shades of cheer,
Until a bird steals off the beer.
We laugh it off, it's all in jest,
In this fine grove, we are all blessed.

The sun dips low, the shadows play,
As we recount our funny day.
Life's little quirks, they give delight,
In coconut corners, life feels right.

Songbirds in a Blazing Sky

In a cacophony of wings and tunes,
The sun starts melting, like sweet balloons.
With every chirp, they start their show,
While tourists try to dance and flow.

A seagull swoops, takes Tim's last fry,
And off he flies, oh me, oh my!
While locals chuckle, full of glee,
They bring us joy, so wild and free.

The rhythm of the waves doth hum,
As beach balls bounce with a happy thrum.
We become the jesters of the land,
With laughter painted in the sand.

So join the song, in this warm embrace,
For every flub is part of the race.
With songbirds bold in azure heights,
We'll own the stage of summer nights.

Intimate Whispers of the Breeze

The wind it tickles, sneaky breeze,
It dances through the swaying trees.
As we sip drinks and share a grin,
It steals our hats; oh where've they been?

From leafy shadows, rumors fly,
Of mermaids giggling in the sky.
The seafoam splashes, playful tease,
While crabs do the cha-cha near the knees.

With shells and stars our treasure maps,
We trade tall tales of silly mishaps.
As twilight calls, we play around,
In this wild world, joy is abound.

So let's embrace this fun romance,
With breezy whispers, we'll take a chance.
In secret corners of balmy nights,
Life's silly wonders spark delights.

Waves of Colorful Twilight

Bouncing beach balls in the air,
A parrot tries to sing a square.
The sun dips low, a disco ball,
Even crabs are dancing at the sprawl.

Flip-flops flying, what a scene,
Here comes a cat in a speedo keen.
Seagulls squawking, calling out loud,
As mermaids giggle in the crowd.

Bananas worth their weight in gold,
Waves crash softly, stories unfold.
Surfboards wobble, folks on parade,
A turtle's joke, a real charade!

Sunset paints the sky with glee,
As we sip coconuts by the spree.
Laughs echo, the night's just begun,
On this beach, we're all just one.

Serenade of the Sunlit Isles

A hula hoop made of a vine,
Pineapples dance, oh how they shine!
The sun winks through palm tree shade,
While too much sunscreen's been applied.

Crabs hold a conga line so bold,
While odd-shaped shells tell tales of old.
Jellyfish giggle in the bay,
As starfish trumpet the end of day.

Coconuts debating with the breeze,
On who has the best dance moves with ease.
A salsa class with lizards galore,
All the while, we laugh and implore.

Under a blanket of twilight's fun,
The moon peeks out, the day is done.
With twinkling laughs that light the space,
We share our hearts in this wild place.

Beneath the Mango Canopy

Mangoes drop like heady dreams,
A monkey joins in with his screams.
Lizards sunbathe on old rusty bikes,
While ants organize their food hikes.

Hammocks sway, a gentle tease,
With snoring friends beside the trees.
Mushrooms giggle, sprouting all around,
As they whisper secrets of the ground.

A bird drops fruit, but it's a bit sour,
And fairies dance over every flower.
Worms play tag beneath the leaves,
Their laughter causing us to freeze.

In this green world, we have our play,
With every moment, we drift away.
As shadows stretch and whispers blend,
We find our joy without an end.

Secrets of Lagoon Reflections

Rippling waters with fish in hats,
Jumping jests from playful brats.
The lagoon serves cocktails so bright,
With umbrellas dancing in the light.

Frogs croak songs with lopsided beats,
While turtles bob to silly feats.
A pelican juggles to impress,
With clams that clap in pure madness.

Sun-kissed dreams float on a raft,
As we share our best goofiest craft.
The stars in the sky join in our cheer,
Shimmering secrets, so bold, so near.

At dusk, the lagoon holds a party supreme,
As we laugh and dance in our whimsical dream.
With echoes of giggles in the moon's glow,
We share this love, and our spirits flow.

www.ingramcontent.com/pod-product-compliance
Lightning Source LLC
Chambersburg PA
CBHW072219070526
44585CB00015B/1403